Presented to

PICKERING & INGLIS LTD. PRINTED IN GREAT BRITAIN

In the same series in paperback

THREE SECRET SEEDS
Joyce Reason

THE BIRTHDAY PLAN
Elisabeth Batt

THE FIRE ESCAPE
Joyce Reason

JOHNNY'S STOLEN PET
Christine Wood

THE ROYAL CARAVAN
Constance Savery

and other titles

A companion series, Junior Gateway hardbacks, is also available.

JAMIE ON HIS OWN

ELISABETH BATT

Illustrated by Daphne Rowles

LUTTERWORTH PRESS
GUILDFORD AND LONDON

First paperback edition 1972
Second Impression 1976

ISBN 0 7188 1943 8

Printed in Great Britain
by Fletcher & Son Ltd, Norwich

Contents

"Don't touch!" (*page 43*)

CHAPTER

I

The Two Houses

JAMIE blinked hard, and pressed his lips together.

"When will you be back, Dad?" he asked, in a very shaky voice.

"To-morrow night. After you're in bed," Dad said cheerfully—just as if he didn't know that to-morrow was Saturday.

All through the week, Jamie looked forward to Saturday. It was not that he didn't like school. But—what was the point of Saturday, if Dad wasn't there?

Dad did something to the car, then wiped his hands on a rag.

"You don't think I *want* to go, do

you?" he demanded, turning to his small son. "But that's the worst of my job; I have to go where I'm sent . . . and I can't come back till the job's done!"

"Had you forgotten that it's S-saturday to-morrow?" quavered Jamie.

"No, of course I hadn't forgotten. And though I'm sorry not to be with you, yet I'm glad you'll be at home all day, because I'm relying on you to look after Mum."

Jamie glanced up at the bedroom window. He could hear Mum up there, putting Lindie, his baby sister, to bed.

"How can I look after Mum?" he asked doubtfully.

Dad hugged him, then got into the car and switched on the self-starter. "Try to help her all you can," he said. "You'll be the only man here, while I'm away. And I'm counting on you."

Jamie felt several inches taller, as he went back into the house. He almost wished that Dad was going to be away for longer. One day wasn't really long enough to show what he could do.

"Mum!" he shouted up the stairs. "What can I do to help you?"

Mum came to the top of the staircase, her finger to her lips.

"Sh!" she cautioned. "I've just got her off to sleep." She came half-way down the stairs and said: "You could feed the chicks for me. Give them one handful of grain each, and one over for luck!"

"What about the two mother-hens, and Percy Porker?" asked Jamie.

"I'll feed them myself, as soon as I've finished up here," she replied.

Jamie filled an old tin with grain from a sack in the kitchen, and took it out into the garden. Jamie's mother had grown up on a farm, and she liked having animals to look after. So Dad had put up a hen-house and wire-run at the far end of the garden; and he had built a little house for the pig, Percy Porker. Just now, there were two broody hens sitting on eggs, in home-made coops. Jamie and his mother were counting the days till the eggs would hatch out.

The two mother-hens poked their heads out through the wooden slats, and made grumbling broody noises when they saw the others being fed. "It'll be your turn, soon," Jamie told them. He found three very brown eggs in the nest-box, and laid them carefully in the tin.

Jamie looked at the big apple-tree. It was a very old tree and didn't bear much fruit, but it was splendid for climbing. Underneath it lay a big pile of sticks and pieces of board, ready for the tree house which Dad had promised to build, up in the apple-tree. They were to have started work on it to-morrow. But with Dad away, he would have to wait a whole week for his tree house.

"Mum," he said later. "Do you know how to make a tree house?" His mother had just fed the pig, after letting the two broody hens out for a few minutes of freedom.

"I've never even seen one," she confessed.

"I don't see why I shouldn't just start it," Jamie said.

"I'd wait, if I were you," his mother advised. "Dad says the important thing is to have a good solid foundation. Otherwise the first strong wind would bring the house down with a crash . . . and you, too, if you happened to be in it!"

"What's a foundation?" Jamie wanted to know.

"Run up and get ready for bed,"

Mum said, "and I'll show you what I mean in your Bible picture-book."

When Jamie had finished his prayers, he said: "Dad said I must look after you, and I'm going to help you to-morrow, all day long."

"I'll like that," Mum said. "There are lots of things you could help me with. But mind you ask the Lord Jesus to help you; otherwise you'll find that everything will go wrong."

Then she opened the Bible picture-book. There was a verse from the Bible, a picture, and a story, on each page.

This was the verse for that night:

"EXCEPT THE LORD BUILD THE HOUSE, THEY LABOUR IN VAIN THAT BUILD IT."

The picture below was in two parts. The first part showed a very pretty house. It stood on the banks of a great river; and on the other side of the river a man was building another house, more solid-looking than the finished one.

"I like that house," remarked Jamie,

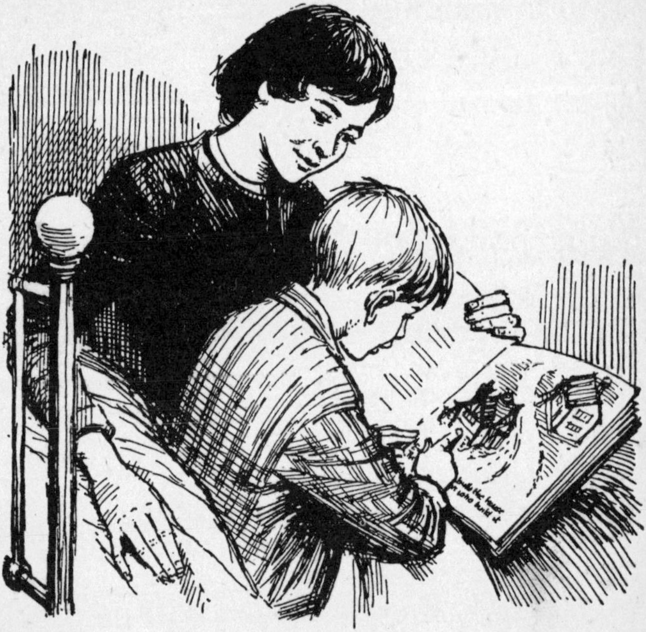

pointing to the first one. "But what does the verse mean?"

"It means that we need God's help in everything; and if we try to do anything without Him, it will come to grief. That man, who hasn't yet finished his house, took the trouble to dig right down till he reached some hard rock . . . and he started building his house from there. The walls go right down into the earth, as far as the layer of rock; that's what is called a good foundation."

"But the other house is *finished*," Jamie pointed out.

"The man who built that one thought he knew best, and he didn't bother about a foundation. He didn't dig down deep at all; he just stuck it on top of the sandy ground. It *looks* all right; but see what happened when there was a storm!"

The second part of the picture showed the ruins of the first house being washed away by the flooded river; while the second house, completed now, stood solid and firm.

"The Lord Jesus said that the man whose house fell down is like the silly people who think they can get on without His help," Mum explained. "But the man whose house stood firm is like the ones who trust in Jesus and ask Him to help them."

Jamie was still studying the pictures. "I remember when the builders started Mr. Baker's new house," he said thoughtfully. "They dug quite deep trenches . . . and began the walls ever such a long way underground. But—we can't do that with a tree house."

"No, but I think Dad knows a way of making a firm foundation even though it's up in the air," Mum said. "Anyway, we'll ask him, when he comes home."

CHAPTER 2

A Bad Start

IT was still dark when Jamie got up next morning. He switched on the light, opened his door very very quietly, and tiptoed down the stairs. Now he was going to make some tea, and take it up to his mother. Dad had been doing this ever since Lindie's teething had been giving Mum disturbed nights. Jamie had helped him one morning, so he knew exactly what to do.

He switched on the electric kettle, being careful not to put too much water in it, so that it wouldn't take long to boil. Then he put the teapot and a cup and saucer on a little tray. He would take up a whole pot of tea, so that Mum could have two cupfuls . . . or three or four, if she liked.

He dipped a little jug into the bowl of milk, and put that on the tray too, and laid two lumps of sugar in the saucer. By the time he had spooned some tea into the pot, the kettle was making a cheerful hissing sound, so he guessed the water must be boiling.

He filled the teapot, then carried the tray upstairs. He went up slowly, one step at a time, so as not to make any noise. If Lindie woke, there would be no more peace for Mum.

He had to balance the tray with one hand, propping it against himself, while carefully turning the door-handle. He managed to get the door open with hardly a sound; but as he went through it, all the contents of the tray slid to one side. He tried to right it . . . but the cup and saucer, teapot and milk-jug behaved as if they were alive! A moment later, the whole tray had slipped out of his hands and fell with a crash to the floor.

With a startled cry, Mum sat up and switched on her bedside lamp, while a series of loud wails came from Lindie's cot. Jamie's mother had been sound asleep, having had to get up several times during the night to quiet Lindie. But when she saw Jamie's dismayed face, she jumped out of bed and ran to him.

"Never mind, darling," she said, as she collected the bits of broken china. "Just run and get a cloth to mop up the mess." And when he came back with the cloth, she said:

"That's a horrid slippery tray; Dad very nearly had an accident with it yesterday! But Jamie—do you know what time it is?"

"It's about seven, I should think," Jamie replied.

"It's just after four!" Mum told him, as she turned Lindie on to her side, and tucked her in more firmly.

"I'm sorry," Jamie said, unhappily. "And for breaking all those things. . . ."

"Don't worry, pet; it was sweet of you to bring me some tea. Another time, though, ask me about it first, when you want to help."

Jamie had felt grateful to her for being so understanding; but her last words made him feel rebellious. Half the fun of being useful was in doing things on your own. It spoilt everything if you had to ask a grown-up first.

"I'll take these down to the dust-bin," he said rather crossly, picking up the tray full of broken crockery.

"No, leave it here for now, and get back to bed," Mum said, yawning. "You must be so cold . . . and you've no slippers on, you bad boy!"

She went with Jamie to his room next door, so as to tuck him up. But just as he was getting into bed, she turned towards the door and sniffed. "I smell something burning!" she exclaimed.

A horrid smell of burning.

"Jamie! Did you turn the kettle off?"

"I think I . . . I'm not sure," Jamie began; but Mum was already running downstairs, so he got out of bed again and followed her. A horrid smell of burning filled the kitchen. Mum had switched the current off, and was peering into her precious kettle.

"I'm afraid it's done for," she said. "You left the current on when the kettle was almost empty, and the element is burnt out."

Jamie turned quite pale. He said nothing, but gazed miserably at his mother.

"I'm not going to scold you," she said, "because I know you were trying to help. But perhaps this will remind you to *ask first* another time."

CHAPTER 3

Poor Lindie!

JAMIE had made a lot of plans for helping his mother. The first one had come to grief; but that made him all the more determined to carry out the rest of them. After his early morning adventures he over-slept, and didn't wake till Mum had got it all ready. He was in such a hurry that he forgot prayers.

However, he cheered up over breakfast, which Mum had made specially nice to make up for his disappointment. And afterwards he helped wash up, made his own bed, and fed the hens.

"You really *have* been useful," Mum said, when he came indoors again. "I don't know what I'd have done without you, because I have to keep going to Lindie."

Poor Lindie had been crying dreadfully. Her gums were hurting her, and now she seemed to have caught cold in one of her eyes. Mum was just wondering whether she ought to take her to the surgery, and, if so, what to do about Jamie's dinner, when old Miss Robbins knocked at the door.

Miss Robbins was their next-door neighbour, and she had come to ask if there was anything she could do to help.

"Would you mind looking at Lindie's eye?" Mum asked her. "She seems to have some sort of infection in it."

"I think you should take her to the surgery, if it gets any worse," Miss Robbins advised. "I don't expect it's anything serious, but it's best to stop that sort of thing in good time."

"We'd have to go by bus," Mum said doubtfully, glancing at the clock. "And

if we have a long wait at the surgery, there's no knowing what time we'll be back."

"If you do decide to go, let Jamie come to me," Miss Robbins said promptly. "I'll give him his dinner, and keep him there till you get home."

"That *is* good of you," Mum said gratefully. "But I don't like to give you all that trouble."

"I'm sure Jamie won't be any trouble," replied Miss Robbins, in her prim voice. "I've got plenty of picture-books and jigsaw puzzles to amuse him. I'll be on the look-out for him; so just send him round to me, if you decide to go."

Soon after Miss Robbins had gone, Lindie dropped off to sleep. Jamie was very glad, not only because he had felt so sorry for her, but also because he didn't want to be left with Miss Robbins. She was kind, but rather fussy, and always treated him as if he were about five years old.

Then, just as Jamie was helping Mum

to peel the potatoes, Lindie woke up and started to cry again.

"I expect she'll drop off if you leave her alone," Jamie said, trying to make his voice sound like Dad's. But after a while Mum had to go to her; and when she came back to the kitchen, she was wearing her going-out clothes.

"I'm sorry, pet, but I think I really ought to take her to the doctor," she said. "Will you go round to Miss Robbins, and say I'll be back as soon as I can?"

Mother wrapped Lindie in a shawl, and put some milk for her and a cheese sandwich for herself in her shopping bag. Before leaving, she locked the door; and she gave the key to Jamie to take to Miss Robbins.

"Ask her to be sure to come and get anything she needs from here," she told Jamie. "I don't want her to go short herself, if she's giving you your dinner!"

She gave the key to Jamie.

Jamie stood outside the garden-gate and waved till Mum and Lindie were out of sight. Then he heaved a deep sigh and began to walk, with dragging steps, towards the next gate. Half-way between the two gates he stopped. There were heaps of things he could do to help, even when Mum was out. She would come home tired, expecting to find a lot of jobs waiting to be done. How glad she would be to find that Jamie had done them all for her! But—she had said: "Go straight to Miss Robbins." Yet, how could he help her if he did that?

Jamie hesitated; then very quickly he went back through his own gate, unlocked the door, and let himself in.

CHAPTER

4

Percy Porker in Mischief

THE first thing he saw in the kitchen was the bowl of peeled potatoes. Even if Mum didn't get home till long after dinner-time, wouldn't she be pleased to find a hot meal waiting for her? He knew which saucepan to use for them, but he was not sure how long they would take to cook. He knew how to switch on the electric stove, though; and having done this, and put the potatoes on to boil, it seemed a pity not to cook something else while he was about it.

He chuckled with delight when he found a small joint of meat in the fridge.

He put it in the meat-tin, shoved it into the oven, and turned on the oven-switch.

This was something like! He would just have to guess about the time. He had seen Mum prod vegetables with a fork to see if they were ready, and he supposed one would do the same with the meat. When Mum came back, they would have dinner together.

Meanwhile, there was a long time to wait, and he was tired of being indoors. There would be plenty of work to get on with in the garden, and he had a suspicion that, in her anxiety this morning, Mum had forgotten to feed Percy Porker and the broody hens.

It was glorious fun mixing the pig-meal, and it smelt simply delicious. The bucket was heavy, and he had to take both hands to it, but first he filled his pockets with grain for the broodies. To save time, Mum usually fed them first, and left them to have their little airing while she fed Percy. By the time Percy had been dealt with, the mother-hens were ready to go back on their eggs.

Jamie felt a little nervous about this part of his work. The hens were such good mothers that they had to be lifted off their eggs. Mum wore thick gloves for this, but he didn't know where they were kept, and they would be too large anyway. It was quite an effort to lift the

broodies out of their coop, and both showed their disapproval by several savage pecks at his bare hands.

"You're being very silly!" he scolded them. "You know you'll make just as much fuss when I put you back again!" It gave him a lovely "big" feeling to be doing real important work, all on his own.

Percy Porker seemed very glad of his dinner. He gobbled it up as fast as it was tipped into the trough; but, as Jamie turned to leave the sty, the pig made a sudden dive through the open door.

Percy was young and active, and he was determined to make the most of his freedom. Jamie chased him round and round the garden till he was breathless. At last he thought he had him cornered; but the pig tried to run between his legs, and Jamie fell flat on his face. When he got up, Percy was nowhere to be seen.

Jamie ran to the gate to make sure

that it was firmly closed. Then he remembered that he had left the kitchen door ajar. This door opened to the garden, and he thought Percy might have taken refuge in the house. But there was no pig in the kitchen, nor in the living-room beyond it.

"Surely he can't have gone upstairs?" Jamie thought desperately. However, he looked into both bedrooms and the bathroom to make sure, before going back to the garden. There was a thick hedge round three sides of it; and since pigs can't fly, Percy must have squeezed through it somewhere.

Jamie went to the part of the garden in which he had last seen Percy, and walked slowly along by the hedge, looking for a hole. Suddenly he heard shrill angry cries, coming from beyond the hedge, on the opposite side of the garden. There, sure enough, was a gap; and Jamie crawled through it into the next-door garden, which belonged to Miss Robbins. Percy was careering about, and Miss Robins was waving a stick and looking very angry.

"Quick! Come and help me! Call your mother!" she gasped. "The brute! He's ruining my plants!"

"I'm awfully sorry," panted Jamie. "He knocked me down . . . that's how he got away."

"Does your mother know he's loose?" demanded the old lady, trying to drive Percy off her rose-beds.

"Mum's not there," Jamie told her, forgetting that if Mum wasn't there he, and not Percy, should have been on this side of the hedge with Miss Robbins.

Miss Robbins remembered, though. "Didn't she tell you to come here and stop with me while she was out?"

"Well—as a matter of fact, I think she did mean me to," Jamie admitted. He added, importantly: "But there was so much work to do, I thought I'd better stay at home."

"You're a very naughty boy——" Miss

Robbins began; but just then Percy decided that he liked his own garden best, and returned to it by the same way he had come. Jamie wriggled through after him; and when Miss Robbins had blocked the hole with a wooden box, she went out through her front gate and in at the one next door.

At last they got Percy into the sty . . . partly, perhaps, because he was hungry after all the exercise, and remembered his unfinished dinner.

Miss Robbins was tired and flustered and worried; and because of this, she felt very cross with Jamie.

"You're a very disobedient boy!" she scolded. "*Why* didn't you come straight to me when your mother left? *Why* did you let the pig out? *Look* at your clothes . . . *and* at your hands and knees!"

She then said that Jamie was to come home with her at once, but that first he must be cleaned up. "I'm not going to have all that dirt brought into my nice clean house," she snapped. She grasped his shoulder and pushed him through the outside kitchen door. But there she paused.

"What's that horrible smell?" she asked. "Did your mother leave something in the oven by mistake?"

She wrenched open the oven door . . . and there was the little joint, burnt nearly to a cinder. The potatoes, too, had boiled dry, and were burning at the bottom of the saucepan.

"It was me," Jamie said miserably. "I started cooking dinner . . . ages ago . . . and forgot—while I was chasing Percy."

He had never felt more like crying; but Miss Robbins was so cross that he soon began to feel cross, too, instead of sorry. She cleared up the mess, and scoured the tin and saucepan without allowing him to help, as if he couldn't be trusted to touch anything. And she took him upstairs and scrubbed his hands and knees, treating him like a baby. Then, after locking the door, she took him to her house.

"I had my own dinner long ago," she said. "But I'll warm up what's left. Now, sit quite still, while I get it ready."

There was steamed fish, which Jamie hated, followed by rice-pudding, which was nearly as bad. But by this time he was so hungry that he managed to eat most of it. Then Miss Robbins made him hold a skein of wool while she wound it into a ball. This was very boring, and he kept letting the skein slip—not always by accident—so that the wool got tangled.

All this time he was thinking of all the real, proper work he might have been doing if he could have stayed at home. But he did not remember the two broody hens which he had left pecking and scratching in the grass near their coops. One was such a good mother that she had gone back to her coop without being told to, and was now sitting tightly on her eggs. But the other had wandered off to another part of the garden, while her eggs were getting colder and colder.

CHAPTER

5

In Miss Robbins's House

IT was dreadfully dull in Miss Robbins's house. There were lots and lots of ornaments and framed photographs, and Jamie would have quite liked looking at them, but Miss Robbins kept saying: "Careful, dear!" and "Don't touch!" and "Don't shuffle your feet, dear; it wears out the carpet."

He soon tired of the jigsaw puzzle she had given him; and then there was nothing to do but look at picture-books while she knitted. After a time he stopped even trying to be good, and said something rude to Miss Robbins every time she said "Don't." When she said:

"I know a little boy who is being Very Silly!" he stood on the sofa and jumped up and down, shouting: "Silly yourself! Silly yourself!"

He sat down at last because he sud-

denly realized that he was very tired. It *was* tiring to sit still and do nothing.

"Can't I go out in the garden?" he asked.

"No, you must stay where I can see you. You've shown that you can't be trusted," was the reply.

He muttered something rude, but Miss Robbins went on knitting, pretending not to hear. But after a few minutes she said: "I'm afraid I shall have to tell Mother what a naughty little boy I've had here."

Then Jamie felt even less like trying to be good. Yet . . . if he now behaved extra-specially well for quite a long time, perhaps Miss Robbins would forget to tell Mum what had happened before?

But—oh dear! It seemed as if he had forgotten how to behave nicely. Whatever he did turned out wrong; even when he meant it to be good, it came out bad.

He didn't notice how tired Miss Robbins looked, nor how often she glanced at the clock. He only knew how tired and cross and miserable he was himself.

When, really without meaning to, he was rude again, she said: "Mother is going to feel very sad when she hears about this. And whatever will she say when she finds all that good food wasted . . . and sees the damage the pig has done in the garden?"

It was when she said this that Jamie suddenly remembered the two mother-hens!

"Miss Robbins!" he exclaimed. "I must go home quick. I've done something terrible."

"What is it now?" she asked wearily.

"The mother-hens!" he shouted. "I forgot to put them back in their coops. The eggs will be cold!"

"You naughty boy! Why did you let

them out?" she demanded. "Come back, Jamie . . . come here *at once*. You can't go home till Mother comes."

"But the eggs . . . the little chickens were to hatch out next week. If the eggs are cold, there'll be no baby chickens."

He burst into tears; and though Miss Robbins knew nothing about broody hens, she fetched her coat and followed him to his own garden.

The good hen was sitting on her eggs as if she had never left them. The other was still scratching for food in the vegetable-patch . . . and all her eggs were stone-cold.

Jamie cried and cried. The tears streamed down—all those tears he had kept back during the unhappy disappointing afternoon.

And then—suddenly Mum was there! Miss Robbins and Jamie both started trying to explain what had happened;

but she only said: "Wait till I've put Lindie in her cot. Yes, she's quite all

right. The doctor gave me some ointment for her eye."

When Lindie was tucked up in bed, Mum said: "How long has the hen been away?"

There was silence for a moment. Then Miss Robbins said: "I'm afraid Jamie has been very naughty and disobedient. He stayed here alone after you had gone, and got up to all kinds of mischief. He disturbed the sitting hens . . . and he let the pig loose. You should see the state my garden's in!"

Mum looked at Jamie. "And I trusted you!" she said.

"And he's been playing about in the kitchen, and ruined your joint," Miss Robbins continued. "I'd no idea he was here by himself. As soon as I knew you'd gone, I took him to my house."

"I hope he was a good boy while he was with you?" Mum asked anxiously.

"Well, no; I'm sorry to say he—he wasn't," Miss Robbins replied unwillingly. She had turned very red, and if she hadn't been old Jamie would have thought she was trying not to cry.

Mum said: "Stay here, Jamie." She took the old lady's arm and said: "You look as if you have a headache. I'm *so* sorry this has happened."

As they went out through the gate, Miss Robbins was saying: "I expect it was my fault, really. I know so little about boys." When Jamie heard that, he stopped feeling cross with her because she had called it "getting up to mischief" and "playing about", when he had tried to do Real Work. He just felt very, very sorry.

CHAPTER 6

Building the House

WHEN Mum came back, she said: "It's a great pity about that sitting of eggs. But I'm much more sad about you, Jamie. And poor Miss Robbins!" Mum went on. "She was too kind to say much; but she looked so upset, I guessed you'd been unkind to her."

Jamie thought of the stuffy little room, "It was awful there!" he mumbled.

"We all have to put ourselves out for other people sometimes," Mum told him sternly. "Miss Robbins is old and not very strong. *She* put herself out to help us; couldn't *you* have put up with a little dullness?"

"I didn't mean to be naughty with her," Jamie explained. "At least, not all of the time," he added truthfully. "But

even when I tried to be good, it sort of came out as badness."

Mum looked as if she understood what

he meant. "If you've been sitting still all afternoon, you'd better go out in the garden for a bit, before you go to bed," she said. "I've got to try and think of something to give Dad for his dinner to-morrow." And that was all she ever said about the spoilt meat and potatoes.

Jamie wanted to ask if he could feed the hens and collect the eggs. But he felt shy about offering to help after all the blunders he had made. He ran up and down the path several times to let off steam. Then he went to the big apple-tree and looked up at the sort of platform of branches which Dad had said was the very place for a tree house.

"I don't see why I shouldn't just *start* it," he thought. Everything had gone wrong that day, so far. It would be nice to make up for it, by doing something really grand and difficult, like building the house by himself. Dad would be so surprised!

He climbed up with a piece of board; went down for another, and then another, till he had collected several of them. He laid them together to make a floor, and went down again for some sticks to make a framework for the walls. Then he found that he needed string to tie them together; but when he went to the kitchen, Mum was upstairs with Lindie. He found her ball of string, and cut off some lengths with the kitchen scissors. When he was up in the tree again, he tied one end of the stick level with the "floor" he had made; then reached up to tie the other end to a higher branch. He was standing on the "floor", which wobbled a good deal, so that it was difficult to knot the string securely.

"This floor doesn't seem to be quite

firm enough," he muttered, and moved his feet so as to get into a better position. And then—the board he was standing on tipped sideways. Jamie grabbed at a branch, missed it, and fell to the ground with a bump. When his mother came out, a moment later, he was lying under the tree with most of the boards on top of him.

She was afraid that he had hurt his head, but it turned out that he was only "winded". After he had been sick, he managed to breathe properly. But he still felt funny, and was glad of Mum's arm when he walked into the house and up the stairs.

She helped him to undress and wash, and then asked: "Would you like me to help you say your prayers?" And then Jamie remembered. "I never said prayers this morning," he confessed.

"Oh, darling! How could you forget?"

Mum exclaimed. "Have you been through the whole day without asking the Lord Jesus to help you?"

"I forgot all about Him," Jamie admitted. "I suppose that's why . . . why everything went wrong."

"Forgetting God was the most wrong thing of all," Mum told him sadly. She looked as if she minded this much more than the broken tea-things or the burnt kettle; more than the wasted food, and the eggs which now would never turn into baby chicks.

"I'm sorry! Please don't be sad," Jamie whispered.

"You must tell Jesus you're sorry," she replied. "Just think how sad you have made *Him*"*!*

She didn't talk to him any more that evening, as he still looked flushed and drowsy after his fall. But just before he went to sleep, he murmured: "I think I know . . . why I tumbled . . . out of the tree. I must have been standing . . . on something . . . that wasn't . . . quite strong enough."

CHAPTER

7

A New Start

THE next day, as soon as Dad was alone with Jamie, he said: "What have you been up to?"

Jamie stared at the floor and shuffled his feet. "Didn't Mum tell you?" he asked.

"No; I expect she knew I'd rather you told me yourself. We can both trust you to tell the truth, however hard it is." At the word "trust", Jamie turned very pink.

"She trusted me to go to Miss Robbins, but I stayed here alone," he mumbled. "I tried to do things to help . . . but they all went wrong. And when Miss Robbins took me to her house, it—it was awful there, and—and—I was awful, too."

Dad looked very grave.

"Have you told her you're sorry?" Then, as Jamie shook his head: "We'd better go and tell her so, now. That is, if you really *are* sorry?"

"Oh yes—I am!" Jamie said. And when they went next door and he had said what he had come to say, Miss Robbins was so kind and nice that he felt sorrier than ever.

When they were at home again, Dad asked: "How did things go wrong, when you tried to help Mum?"

Jamie screwed up his face, trying to remember. The whole of yesterday had been such a mountain of misfortunes, it wasn't easy to get them in their right order.

"Well, first I got up at four o'clock, by mistake," he began. "And I broke the tea-things, and woke Lindie, and burnt the electric kettle. Then . . . I stayed here alone, like I told you; and I

spoilt the meat and potatoes, trying to cook dinner. And I forgot the mother-hens, so one lot of eggs got cold and won't ever hatch out. And Percy Porker got loose while I was feeding him . . . and

I fell out of the apple-tree when I was trying to build the tree house. . . ."

"No wonder Mum looked tired," Dad remarked grimly. "However did you manage to get in such a muddle, Jamie? You're usually such a sensible chap."

"Mum said . . ." Jamie began; he looked at his shoes, then at Dad's shoes, then out of the window.

"Yes? What did Mum say?" Dad prompted gently.

"She said . . . the most wrong thing of all was . . . forgetting prayers."

Dad was silent for a few minutes. "And what do *you* think?" he asked then.

"I think—perhaps—that's why—all the rest of the day was a muddle," Jamie admitted.

"Does it remind you of something in your Bible picture-book?" Dad asked. Jamie thought for a moment.

"Yes! The two houses!" he exclaimed. "I suppose I've been like the man who built a house without something firm underneath."

"And what happened to the house when there was a storm?"

"It fell to pieces," Jamie remembered. "Mum said it's like a silly person who tries to get on without the Lord Jesus to help. Oh dear—it's just like me, isn't it?"

"But you see, now, what was wrong," Dad said. "What would you do, if you were the man whose house fell down?"

After a long think, Jamie said: "I'd have to clear up the mess, first. But I'd need help over that, wouldn't I?"

"Yes; that part is when you tell our Lord you're sorry, and ask Him to forgive you," Dad explained. "He washes away the bad things, and gives you a new start."

"Then—I'd start to build again, but on firm ground, this time," Jamie continued.

"Yes; a new start isn't any good unless you ask the Lord Jesus to live in your heart, and help you at every moment of the day," Dad told him. "That's like building on firm ground; and it says in the Bible: 'That Rock was Christ'."

Then they went out into the garden. The night had been windy, and all the rest of the boards in the apple-tree had slid to the ground. The upright stick had slipped out of the string, and was dangling from one of the lower branches. Jamie's face grew hot as he looked at the babyish muddle he had made of it.

Then Dad said: "I haven't told you my good news. I'll be getting home early to-morrow afternoon, because of having worked all Saturday. As soon as you're back from school, we'll start work here."

"So we won't have to wait till next Saturday!"

"No, we'll get going with the tree house to-morrow. And we'll begin by making a good solid foundation, so that whatever the weather does, it'll be as firm as a rock."